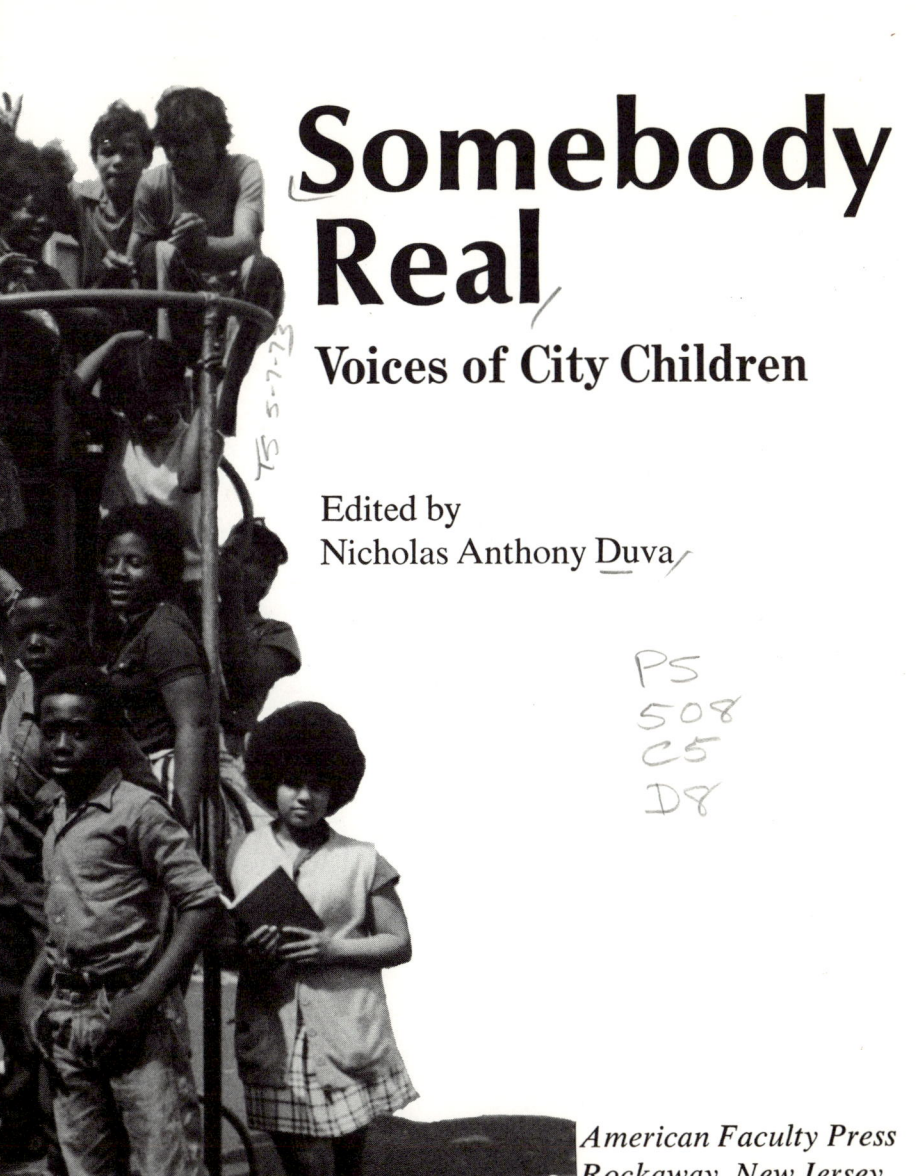

Somebody Real

Voices of City Children

Edited by
Nicholas Anthony Duva

American Faculty Press
Rockaway, New Jersey

for my JANET
who is beautiful in every way

Copyright © 1972 by Nicholas Duva
All rights reserved.
This book or parts thereof may not be reproduced in any form without written permission of the publishers.
ISBN #0–912834–01–3
Designed by Chet Kadish
Manufactured in the United States of America

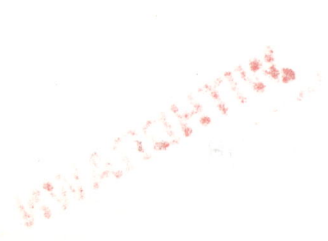

Contents

	Introduction	v
I.	Kevin, Aida, Zaida	1
II.	Betsy	21
III.	Charlene, Olga, Shonda	45
IV.	Ronald	69
V.	Jesus, Debra, Eusebio	87
VI.	Ramon, Eida, Michele, Gil	109
VII.	Jose L., Cheryl, Jose R., Della	127
VIII.	Rosemary	147
IX.	Randy, Priscilla, Darlene, Jackie	161
	Afterword	183

Introduction

In the presentation of a collection such as this, the writings of city school children, I was tempted to call upon what have now become almost standardized epithets for the city and its people—the deprived, the underprivileged, the slum. These pages could easily be used to arouse anger, evoke sorrow, cause concern. We could sigh our way from page to page and, when we are through, promise ourselves to "do something" for "those children" as soon as we get the chance . . .

We all have feelings such as these—odd tangles of pity and fear—when we think of the city. But these feelings are, for the most part, stored away to be called upon in such times that we may feel the need to be immediate, involved, and relevant.

This is not the book to fill that need. The words on these pages are strong, and proud. They reflect not only the pathos, but the warmth, and the music of being 11 or 12 and walking, talking, living, caressing, and hating the city streets. The children are telling us about their lives, and ask no more than our attention—not love, because love would demand too much; not involvement, for the streets are too crowded already; and certainly not pity, which is as out of place as it is out of style in the city.

But if you would listen, really listen, to the words of these children, you would know them. There would then be no need for involvement, no need for love, or pity; for we would feel the pride, the strength in their voices, and walk away with a knowledge of the children that buries any preconceived opinions we may have had about them. We would know them, which is all they really ask.

The children who have contributed to this book have not, however, escaped the terrors of the city, which remain for them a physical and quite penetrating reality. Drugs, and poverty, and immobility is all about them. But a world such as this does not breed despair in everyone. To some, especially to the children, it brings skill, and power, and a firm and dedicated pursuit of warmth, and peace. These children can withstand extraordinary stress—they have all their lives. For their survival, they were made of tougher stuff; tougher, more resilient, more flexible material than most of us. And it shows through.

This anthology was written entirely by the 24 children in Room 312, my self-contained sixth grade class, during the 1970–71 school year. All are black or Puerto Rican, all live in a district of lower Jersey City stricken with the typical city ills—from the crumbling tenements, to the crumbling dreams. But their school is new and real, and most come to it proudly.

Sometime in 1969, an ancient schoolhouse was replaced by a new one, a block-square expanse of brick and glass; but the neighborhood, and its squalor, was left intact. So out of the tenements, onto the glass-strewn streets, past the fences decorated with the curse words and the peace signs, past the tires and the sticks, and the sneakers dangling from the telephone wire, the children of the city walk to school.

These are the writings of those children, They are sometimes joyous, sometimes sad; sometimes angry, and often very, very quiet. But they are all strong, all reflective, all potent and real. The children tell us about themselves, and all they ask is our attention.

Listen to them. Know them.

NICHOLAS DUVA
Jersey City, 1971

I. Kevin, 11; Zaida, 12; Aida, 11

". . . Being something is very hard on you."

BEING ME

I am happy just being me. And also I feel good just doing whatever I want. What I do is a part of me, even the silliest things. No matter what I say or do, I am still the same person.

And I am glad what I am.

—Aida

GOOD AND BAD

It is both good and bad in the city.

It's sometimes dirty, but mostly clean. And everything is nice and colorful like the people and their clothes. There are big new buildings, and sorry burned out and knocked down ones.

And there are people walking and drinking and having babys, and getting hurt in actsdens. And sometimes people get stolen on my block. Nice people, too.

—Zaida

DARK MAN

Not able to be seen. Can't make out. Treading through the night, not able to be seen. Can't see a thing but the white of his eyes and his teeth. Sucked into the night, no way out.

Sneaking around, running from everything white, light, bright, and colorful.

DRUGS

Dope is something
that can knock you out.
Dope is something
that can kill you.

It just takes you in,
and kind of sends you
out and out.

—Kevin

SICK OF IT

I was mad
because I saw
a fight.
Another fight
like the one last night
like the one tonight.
And I'll be mad tomorrow too
they'll fight again—
I want to move.

TROUBLE FOR NOTHING

 Some kids steal cars and steal money from other people, and the first thing you see is the police. And the police stop in front of your house and start talking to you, and the real robbers are just standing in the crowd, laughing.
 And so you get in trouble for somebody else, and you can't tell nobody.
—Zaida

ESCAPE

There are some times when I have to escape from my house and my family. They bother me a lot there sometimes. So I just go across the street and listen to the men argue outside the bar.

—Zaida

FUTURE

My future is ahead of me.
I can never tell
what's going to happen to me,
and I never will.
What I think is
that I will die someday,
and I'll just
fade away.

DRY

I hate to think
Without a drink
Of water.

—Aida

THE SCHOOL BOOK

I had this book,
This terrible book,
Full of history and other old things.

It was bad,
But I had
To read it.

And I didn't like it a bit.

RUN AWAY

I left the projects
and wanted to stay,
but came back home
yesterday.
I had no place to go,
anyway.

—Zaida

NOT WORTH IT

If to be rich
is not so much,
if to be poor
is really hell,
if a side of pretty
is ugly as sin,
if a side of bad
is really nice,
if everything is fake—
it's not worth it
to be anything.

    I like my grandmother Ella and my uncle Willie Frank just as much as I like my mother, father, brothers and sisters. They can get me happy completely.
—Kevin

LUNCH

I like lunch.
I like the bunch,
And the crunch,
Of my friends around me.

ME

I am not really a poor girl no different than other not really poor girls. I am not special from others.

Sometimes people bother me with their mouth, but I don't care because this is only words. Sometimes I am happy, like when I get out of school, because when I get home I see my mother. And I am really happy because I got a mother, because she's the only one I got to care, because I love her like she love me.

My mother told me that if I get promoted and don't have to go to summer school, I get a round trip to P.R. for the summer and maybe forever. Because she loves me and don't want me to get hurt or anything around here this summer.

—Zaida

ABOUT ART

Art can really sneak up on you. Especially for an artist. If one thing don't go right for him, he is just going to give his self a hell of a time. And more. He just might kill his self. If he's really an artist, you never know. That crazy fool artist of his self. He just might. Art can do that to you.

GRANDFATHER

My grandfather is dead,
And is gone.
My grandfather is dead,
And is past away.
He is just dead,
And very deep in dirt.

But his life and his whole self is OK,
And safely put away.

—Kevin

PLAYING

I saw kids playing
with old tires,
and boards,
and ropes.

And when they finished with that,
only half the day was gone
with nothing else to do.

MY FRIEND

I have a friend,
not a good friend,
not smart, or cute, or anything.

But she's a friend,
the only one around,
so she'll do.

—Zaida

WHAT GOD DID TO CREATE US KIDS, WOMEN, AND MEN

Well, I think that god had some kind of chemicals to create us. That's what I think. But I know, I'm sure, that what he did was a special, special, specialist thing. A thing you can't buy, or find anywhere. And when he created us kids, women, and men, that is what he used.

He is the only one with these special things. He makes them, and he keeps them in his refrigerator so they don't go bad. That's just got to be it. I almost know that it is. And I will never forget it as long as I live.

FACES

Faces are pretty,
Some are ugly.
Sometimes they're the disgrace of the body.
God don't care,
But faces mean a lot
To people.

—Kevin

NO PLACE

I have no home
And am all alone
In this world of make believe.
I have no place to go
And I'll never
Get away.

DEAD

I can hardly think.
My mind is about to sink.
If I think any harder,
Things will only be farther.
I've got to stop,
And sleep.

—Aida

AFRAID

I hate to look at my cracked floor,
Because it makes me look so poor.
And it feels,
To me,
Like an open door.

THE KNIFE

There was this knife,
It stopped a life.
It let his blood flow,
And his life go.
I saw this Saturday.

—Kevin

SLEEP

Asleep one night,
I saw a bright light.
It bounced inside my head,
And I heard a sound like a deep hole.

MY WISH

Would I like to be in P.R. right now! There it's so nice and hot, and here it's so cold. And if I would be there, I probably be swimming in the river instead of drowning in school.

—Zaida

TO LOVE

Well to really love is not just to kiss or do that thing. It is to come upon some girl or boy, talk to each other, rap on to each other. Do your thing, tell her or him what's going on in your mind, how you feel, what you think about love. What goes on in your heart, will you go on with your thing, will you quit it. How you like things, hot or cold, hard or soft, light or dark, run or stay.

Who knows. Love might just happen to you. You got to look. Love is not to be lost. Love is to be found.

TO PARTY

Party all night, jumping all around,
Doing your thing, doing no kind of harm.
Just party all night, letting your mind go,
Yelling and laughing.

And dance to dance,
Laugh to laugh,
Yell to yell,
Doing no kind of harm.

—Kevin

BEING SOMETHING

Being something
is very hard on you.
You have to do so much,
and try so hard,
and you have to be kicked around,
dropped,
banged around,
and more.

Being something
is very hard on you.

—Kevin

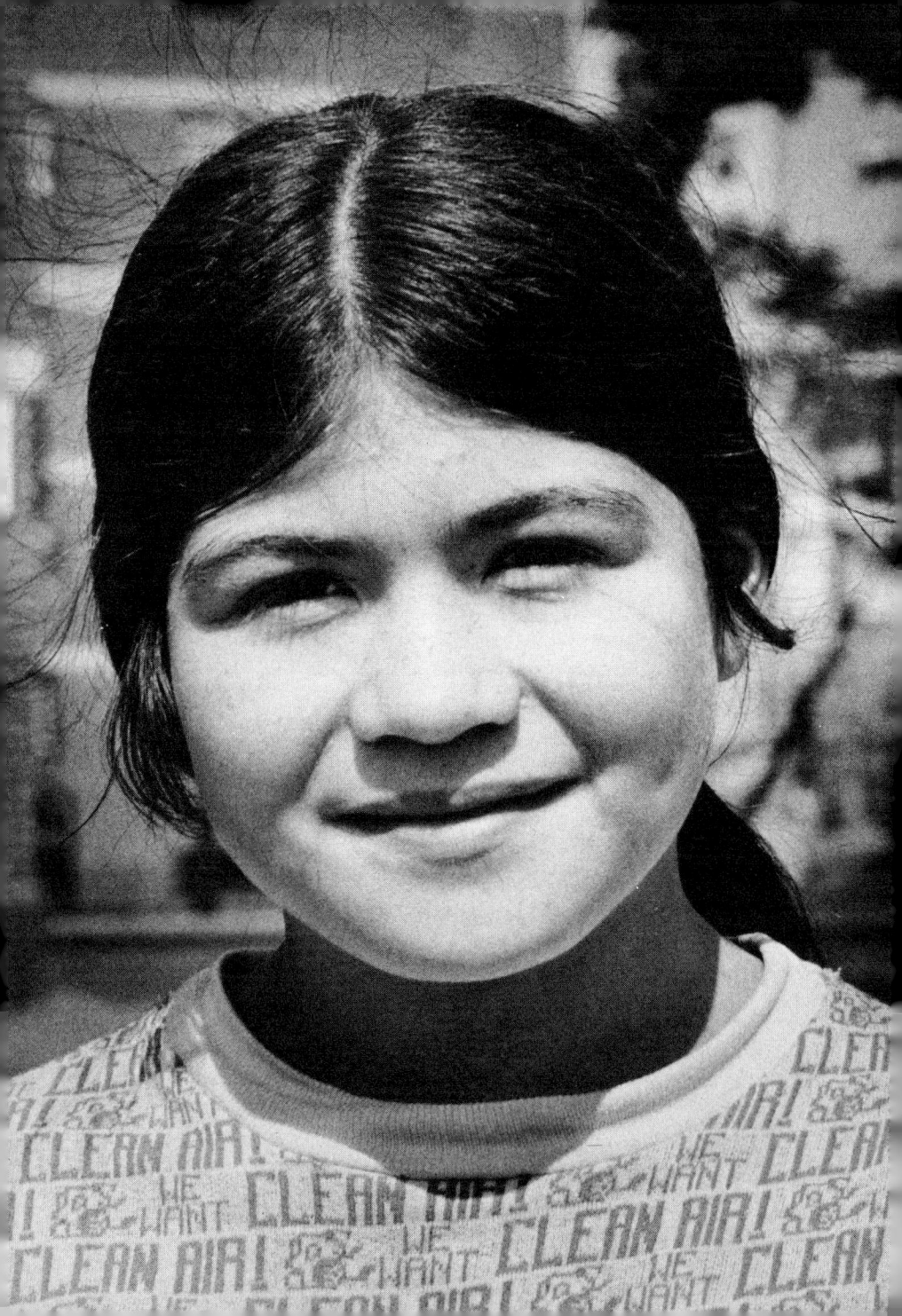

II. Betsy, 11

"Keeping off darkness and deadness as long as I can."

WHY I WRITE

You see, you hear, you think. If you didn't do these, what would you be? So I write because I want the people to know that I am active and willing, not sick and beat up. I write so you can know and see that I am alive. And dangerous.

—Betsy

MINDS

What is happening in people's minds?
They go clickity-clack,
Like blinds.

But no one is thinking of someone—
And others are thinking of themselves.

STORY OF ME

When I was small and chubby and fat,
Doing this, and all of that,
I used to cry for papa.

Now that I am young and free,
I do what pleases me.

But when I am old, and sit and sigh,
Maybe get sick, and maybe cry,
I'll just wait with myself, to die.

THIS WORLD

I think that if this world would stop littering, taking drugs, heroine and everything, it wouldn't be a bad place to stay.

All you see is all the stores broken down, and the police cars and ambulances. The only way to get peace and quiet is when you die.

Where I live is a mess. They robbed a liquir store and all the kids were running out with beer and whiskey and everything. Some littler kids went in too, and took out toilet paper to throw around.

That's what I hate. You see all the blood around the streets. Everything.

A GOOD MORNING

When I woke up this morning, I felt good, like it was spring. Because my aunt came from Puerto Rico with my cousins. And so when I woke up, there was a good smell in the house. It smelled almost like P.R.

THE SECRET

Everybody knows who I am.
Everybody knows what color I am.
Everybody knows how I look.

Everybody doesn't know
That I am dead.

I STAYED

I dreamed I went into this palace, and it was scary at first. I heard somebody coming, and I thought danger was up ahead.

But it was a king. He had a cigar and he had a gentle giraffe by his side. He offered me some juice, and a slice of a cake that he had. I nibbled and tasted on it.

I studied the palace. And I said this palace is as big as all my dreams. I had some baggage and a suitcase, so I stayed. And I never came back again.

A HOT DAY

Today they'll have the pumps on. Yesterday they did, and I got dragged in. But I was refreshed, and the little drops of water felt fine on my face.

So today I'll go under again. And I'll wash my uncle's car if he brings it around.

MY COLOR

White is my color, and I am proud of it. If I was black, I would still be proud.

Some white people, they hate black. And some black, well they hate white. But I like them both. And I am only one. Spanish white.

CLIMATE

The climate in Jersey City was bad,
And people were very, very sad.
They didn't have such a good time,
And they said the fault was mine.
I said I didn't do it.
I screamed I didn't do it.

They were mad a lot, and not a little,
But since music soots the savage beast,
I played the fiddle.
And got off easy.

LEAVING

Soon I am leaving this place and going to heaven to be with god and leave all my troubles behind. Getting my heart full of joy and laughing. Just leaving my other world behind and feeling free to do anything I want. Just like letting myself apart. Leaving every problem I have in the world far, far behind where I can't see them, and they can't see me.

---

outside

ther are riots outside,
they never stop till night,
they shoot, they mug.

you feel sad inside,
but they feel happy.

IN MY DESK

books,
and pretzels,
and a bobby pin—
and wrappers which
my gum came in . . .

THE PRINCE AND THE DRAGON

There was once a prince and a dragon, who lived very happy together. Every time the prince was cold, the dragon burned his fire for him to warm up.

One day the prince's friend from New York came and saw the dragon by the prince. Now he never heard of the dragon because the prince told nobody. This was because everybody was very cold, and the dragon wasn't strong enough to warm everybody.

So the friend kicked the dragon who he thought was burning the prince, and the dragon got so excited that it let out real hot fire and roasted the prince to a crisp. And the prince died with his wonderful secret.

Moral—always share your dragon.

MOVING AWAY

I live in a block where there are a lot of riots and things. Like fights and deaths. I don't like where I live, but I am helpless. My mother always says we will move to York Street, but we never do.

So my sister is starting to find an apartment.

LOVE

Love is a thing of beauty. I can't pit love in words. I have to feel it to know it. I can't just put it in plain words. I got to be loved to say it, and you got to love to hear.

LIFE

what is life?
is it a wife?
is it your kids?
is it chasing what? where? did?

yes, it is all that
plus chocolate dressing, and costume hats,
and a whole lot more.
that's life.

BEATING OURSELF

There's always a fight
at night.
Come one, come all,
come see the big fall
of us all.

NOISE

leaves fall down,
they don't make a sound—
nature is quiet.

windows break,
guns shoot off as robbers take—
people are loud.

WHAT IS HOLLOW?

Hollow is empty,
Hollow is steep.
And it's also deep.

If you look through it,
You see nothing.

THE JUDGE

The judge is a person
Who decides who wins
For people who did wrong things.

But mostly the judge just sits at his table
And looks at his navel.

THE CITY

the city is a waste.
you always have to haste.
the city's so crowded with people,
that you can't see the top of the steeple.
and it just goes on and on.

A CRUMB

A crumb of bread is little,
Some people are crumbs.

But a crumb is small
and it will fall
little by little.

DIFFERENT

What is different?
It's when you're not sick of it.

OLD BAM

There was once an old man around my way, his name was Bam. That wasn't his real name, but they called him that because he always bumped into things. All the people were bumped into by him, too. He was mostly sick, not drunk.

One day he bumped into a tree and went crazy, bumping into tree after tree, and everything else around him. Then after he hit about the 125th thing, he fell on the side walk and he died.

Then all the people went to his funeral and said what a nice old man he was. But they really hated him because they used to make fun of him and all. It's terrible that they should do that.

I hope when I die that they can't find my body.

THE MISTAKE

I looked up a tree
And what did I see?
I saw a rat that looked like a cat.
I took him down, and he gave me a frown
And he bit me and ran away.
Leaving me with nothing to say.

LONELY

To be lonely is to feel empty in your heart with no one near you to comfort you. All you hear is squeaky little noises which you never heard before. And you start getting scared.

But then someone comes and you don't feel lonely, you feel like released from tightness. Then you start comforting whoever came because you thought he or she was lonely for you too. And you both feel happy.

ME

there I was, lying in bed,
saying to myself
where am I
who am I.

I looked for another answer, but there was only one—

I am here,
and I am me.

TASTE ME

Once there was this pencilwith a funny head, and all it could say was taste me, taste me. So a little boy of 6 ate the pencil, and every time he opened his mouth, he would say taste me. So a man of24 came and ate the little boy. And then when he would open his mouth, he would say the same thing. And then an old man ate the man of 24 who ate the boy of6 who ate the pencil.

And this went on until an old, old man ate them all, got endergestion, and died, ending the rain of terror and death.

GOD

God is a person up above
who helps you love.

WHERE I LIVE

Where I live all they do is play ball and steal. They have already stolen 4 cars and wrecked them. The streets are filthy with wrecks around.

But in the summertime when I stay home I can look out a window and hear a lot of people playing at a good time. I hear radios, motorcycles, bells ringing from stores. I hear my friends calling Betsy can you come outside.

But especially you can see the police cars passing by.

DIRTY PEOPLE

There is a boy I like very much,
But I really don't like to touch—
Because they say he has germs,
And if you touch him, he burns.

So this boy that I like so much,
I'll never be able to touch.

FLOWERS

Flowers in the garden,
Flowers in the pot—
No flowers in dirty old yards.
No flowers in broken down houses.
But I'll plant there.
I'll plant so the world can see
That even sorry old houses and dirty yards
Can have flowers,
And be bright again.

BOOKS

Some books are stupid,
Some are good.
Some are sad.
I don't like to read sad books,
Because they make me think
And remember
A tired day.

A SCHOOL THAT I WOULD INVENT

If I could invent a school, I would only put books that are new books. I mean not history, because history was 1604 years ago. I would get teachers that used to be drug attics and let them teach even if the education board says no.

And I would have all the kids who are problems or anything in a special school, not mine. But I really wouldn't do that because then they wouldn't have a chance. Most of them only want to show off in front of everybody. Not really bad. Like Jose.

In my school, the teachers would work only with the dumb kids, and leave the smart kids to learn by themselves. Then the dumb ones can catch up. And I would work, and work, and work so that everyone in the world would be smart.

MY FIGHT

When I'm dead, dead and gone,
What would I see?
Darkness and deadness.
I wouldn't be able to see trees or birds,
Nothing but darkness. And deadness.
But what I am now doing is living,
Seeing all the beauties and the uglies,
Seeing all the world.
This is my fight—
Keeping off darkness and deadness
As long as I can.

—Betsy

III. Charlene, 12; Olga, 11; Shonda, 11

*". . . so you walk away,
trying to believe in yourself."*

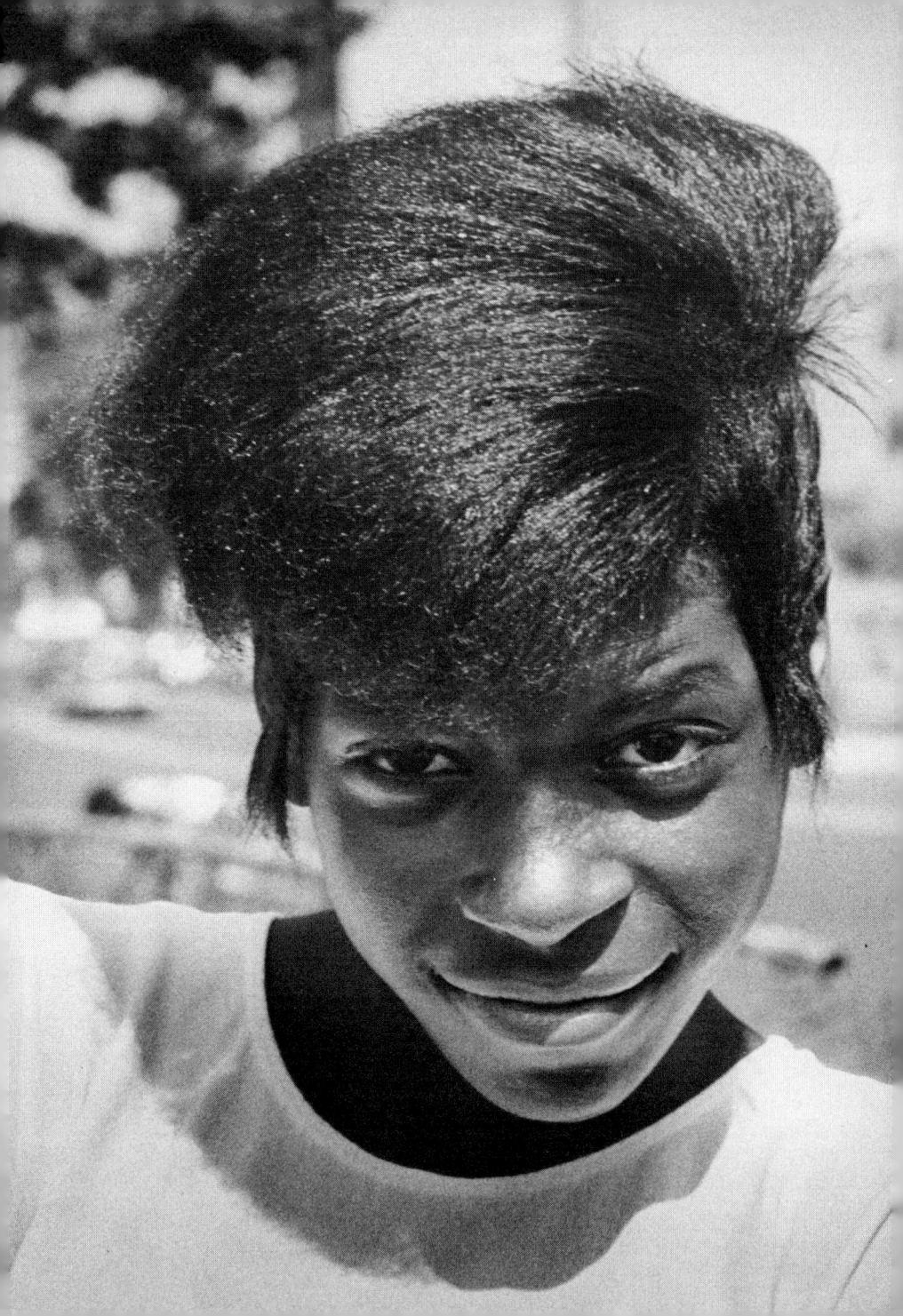

DAYBREAK

The sun comes up,
And shows the dark shadows
Of trash that was left
From yesterday.
It shines in the dingy windows,
Shines past gray rats
Racing across the room.
It shines in the face of a too young mother,
Who sits in a chair
By the door,
Dreaming of something else.
                              —*Charlene*

WHERE

Where am I?
At home, at school, outside?
At times I feel
I am nowhere.

WHAT

What I have,
What I got,
It's nothing like what I want.

—Olga

THE SPIRIT

I am a spirit who once was a person. My life was taken away by someone I didn't even know. It is misurable underneath the cold dirt. While I lay here, bugs bite at me.

Imagine being what I am. You wouldn't like it a bit. You should really try to keep living.

THE WELFARE

Most people are on the Welfare,
And they don't even seem to care.
They get on the bus,
And don't even have carfare.
When I ask them how they dare,
They call me an SB.
Then I talk to them real kind,
Try to get right inside their mind,
But they don't listen because they don't care,
Because they on the Welfare.

—Shonda

BACK TO THE CITY

As we walk along the grassy road,
We spot a pond, lilly pads and a toad.
The sun shining, trees breaking the wind,
But we feel hot, and itchy, and mad at fresh air, so
We go back
To the city.

WHY I WRITE

When I write a poem or a story,
I write it because I feel it.
I mean because,
It either happened to me,
Or I wish it would.

—Charlene

WHEN I TALK

When I am talking english in my spanish way, I think that I am talking wrong. I think that all the people are laughing at me for it. I am sure that I am going nowhere with my talking. That's no lie. I think that when I talk the people don't listen to me for nothing. And my mother says that nobody likes spanish talk and I think that she is right.

MY FRIENDS

One day my shoe got so fulled with dirt that I had to take it off and take out the dirt. My friends took my shoe and threw it away, and when I went to get it, I got stuck in my foot with bottle glass. They took me to the hospital and gave me 7 stiches. And the doctor told me not walk on my foot because it could get infected. That's how good my friends are with me.

—Olga

SADNESS

My life is dull, I have nothing to live for. My grandmother has died before me. My mother was hurt, my father was hurt, and so was all my family. When a person is living, you always desert them. But you always feel bad once they are gone. There's nothing like a person to keep living so you can love them longer.

FOR ME TO DO

When I wake up, I don't know where I'm going.
I look at my mother, and she's busy sewing.
Then by the window, my sister's busy throwing
Paper planes to the wind that's blowing.
I look around the house,
Wondering how to start the day.
— *Shonda*

DEATH

street
shot
strangled
stabbed
dead

NOISE

There's noise about,
And I sit and wonder—
Where is quiet?

—Charlene

FIGHTS

black—white
black—white
that's all the fighters say.
when they fight, they start,
and if they don't say "your mother",
they go back to
black—white
black—white

MY SCHOOL

If I had a school, I would put in it the poorest children who are out begging for help. I'd let some nuns run the school, because they seem to be the most loyal people in the world.

I would try to start kids minds to function. I would teach them, and pray for them. I am poor and they are poor, but we would give everything we had to each other.

—Shonda

WHO?

When I pray, who do I pray to?
When I sing, who listens?
When I laugh or dance, who joins me?

I don't know.
I'm always alone.

SOMEONE SAYS

Someone says "look at her raggy clothes"
Someone else says "she can't afford no better"
You walk away,
Trying to believe in yourself.

—Charlene

SCHOOL IS OUT

Sometimes when school is going on, you want to be out. And when you're out, you want to be in. You've had these troubles before. For instance, when it's the last day of class you're happy, but then after 1 week you get school sick.

Home is just a place to live, work, and get hurt on your way outside from. School is different. You don't have to work, or get hurt, you just learn. No one wants to get hurt, I think. And that is how I feel when school is out.

FRIENDS AND ENEMIES

I am a black man who's been in the war. I was shot in the war, and none of my people came to help me. My feelings were hurt as I was dying and they were leaving me. All of a sudden, my best friend walked up to me and said die friend. Then it hit me. I shot him dead. I turned to my enemy. I threw up my flag, and gave up. I surrendered. Then we were no longer enemies. When we needed help after that, I came to him, and he came to me.

—Shonda

SLEEP

Night time comes, but never sleep,
Summertime air blows through the streets:
Odors,
And noises,
And filthy sights,
But I'm used to it now, so
I fall asleep.

         —Charlene

I AM

I am a person with nothing much to do. But it still seems like I never stop doing things. I always move, but never really get anywhere. People tell me that I am smart, but I really am not. Because I never do things for people. I just do my own work, and mind my own business and that's not really smart. I'm not smart at nothing. Sometimes I have to ask someone how you do the arithmetic.

I THINK

I think I am myself, but sometimes I think I'm not. Then I feel like doing nothing at all. I feel like not coming to school or even breathing much. Not talking. Not anything. Then my mother calls me and so she screams and asks me what I was doing there. I say I was thinking how it must feel to be blacker than just black. I feel this inside myself. It hurts and it won't go away. I hate to think.

—*Olga*

THE CITY VISITOR

Lost in a jungle of throw-out cans,
dirty sidewalks, and drunken men,
he tries to rest, but must await
a mugging or raping, or other fate.

Should he stay there forever?
Will he?
Never!

—Charlene

HATE

I hate the friends
that bother me most,
but I hate any people
that are doing it, doing anything,
just for fun.

LOVE

I loved my friend,
he went away from me.
So this poem ends,
as soft as it began.
I loved my friend.

—*Olga*

THE MAN WANTS TO PLAY

Where I play there's not no swings or anything like that, so we play punch ball in the street. So this man comes up and asks to play and I don't say anything to him. So he goes to my girlfriend, and she says OK. So I say to her if he plays, I don't because that man was a nasty man, he feel girls behind and girls leg and all the stuff that can get you having babys before you should.

WORDS

Words are big,
words are small,
words are funny,
or sad.
But mostly words go in circles
in this funny little world.

—Olga

HOUSES AROUND

Outside my window,
I look and see
Old tenement houses
Looking back at me.
Their furniture stolen,
Their windows all broken,
And I peep in.

—Charlene

WHERE I AM

I like where I am because you can do a lot for people. And someone always needs something, like clothes or money help.

And when you help someone, the whole place changes. Suddenly there are a lot of beaches and the ocean around. Everything looks light and colorful. For instance the buildings become bright, and the markets treat you right.

Right now I am in the City Jail, but as soon as I get out, I am going to explore the world as it is in this new, good way.

—*Shonda*

MY ROOM

When I open my window,
I can hear
everything that goes on
next door.
Their bathroom is next to ours,
and their lights are always going on and off.
Their kitchen is close too,
and as they sit and talk, I can hear
everything so clearly.
Sometimes I don't mind at all,
but when I am tired and sleepy
they talk and yell very loud,
and they keep the lights on.
—Charlene

PEOPLE

I think about people,
people who are sick and old.
But in those thoughts, I am happy to know
that there are people who are healthy,
and willing to live.

TEACHER HATE

I hate when a teacher is grouchy and takes it out on his kids. To get back is not the right thing to do. Making the kids write and write and he sits down and does nothing. That is just plain stubborn. Sometimes when he's wrong, he just don't want to admit it. But it would be the best thing to do. All the kids know what's going on anyway. He shouldn't bring his problems to school. He should leave them back wherever he lives and work on them when he gets there.

—*Shonda*

THE COLOR BLACK

Black is the color of our race.
It is a very bad one.
It always gets hurt, and killed.
I'm glad that I'm black,
But I don't want to get killed—
So I stay
Out of the way
Of my color.

—Shonda

IV. Ronald, 11

". . . I just agree with the ones who I think are right. And that's the best you can do, really."

ME?

Me? I'm grass swaying in the wind. I'm soft and nice and sweet. And I'm black, big and proud. I'm the wind, keeping my cool. I'm a slim, tall tree that was born from nature.

I'm human, with blood and brain. I was born from nature, and I won't forget it. I'm living. I'm a person who can walk, talk, think, touch. Nothing less than human.

I'm somebody. Somebody real.

BOTHERED

When cops bother me for nothing,
I feel angry,
And ready to fight.
I feel that I must kill,
I feel smashing mad.
I can't help it.
I can't stand it.

CITY TIME

City time can be good, and it can be vishous.
City time gives you too much time to do nothing,
and not enough to do what you must.

HAPPY, AND SAD

I feel joyful,
I feel crazy,
I feel nice,
I feel groovy,
When I'm happy.

I feel drousy,
I feel bad,
I feel beat up,
I feel dead,
When I'm not.

HOUSE FIGHT

A fight in your house,
Your mother says go.
You don't know where.
You have to go, out of the house,
Out of the house, out of her sight,
But where?

DARKNESS

You can't see a thing
Your mind is in darkness.
You're alive, and you want to see,
But your darkened mind won't let you.
It just won't let you.

I DON'T KNOW

I don't know about Japan. I don't know about Europe. I don't know about China. All I really know is about Jersey City, and that it is dirty and very sad.

WHERE IS GOD?

Where is god?
Where does he live?
Some people say in heaven.
I don't really know.
I just agree with the ones
Who I think are right—
And that's the best you can do, really.

WHAT I HATE

a tube
with a needle on the end
full of dope.
a gun
with bullets in it
and an easy trigger.
a knife
with a shiny point
ready to kill.
I hate it.

WHAT HAPPENED?

Who started it, and why?
When did they start it, and where?
What happened?

We'll never know.
All we know is someone fled,
And another man is dead.

SADNESS

    This is for real. They never fix the elevator in the projects. Well, one day my sister was coming out of the elevator and it closed too fast and started to go up. And her legs were caught. So she got 2 fractured thighs and 1 broken leg and a lot of cuts all over.
    She is now home in this wheelchair.

MY COLOR

I seem to be black, but I really am brown.
I just feel black.

THE WAY IT IS

Some people are happy,
Some are sad.
Some people are sickly,
Some are mad.
Some go to school,
Some don't.
Some will work,
Some won't.
And that's the way it is.

IF I WERE RICH

If I were rich, I would buy a car for me and my girlfriend. I'd give my mother some money, and my father too. I would also give a little to my sisters and brothers. I would buy a new house, and put carpet in the whole thing, even the halls.

The rest I would save for phone bills and insurance.

LUNCH IN SCHOOL

When I stay in school to eat my lunch,
I have to wait in line.
So I just leave and don't eat lunch,
Just to save some time.

WHAT I LIKE ABOUT WHERE I LIVE

What I like about where I live is that people are nice to you and they care about you. Not like other places. It seems that people are more free here, free to help their people out when they are down.

For instance, if you fall where I live, someone will come along, give you a bandaid, help you up, and carry you to your house. In other places if you fall, people would walk right past you. If you say you need help, and can't get up, they'll wave their hand and say the hell with you.

We also have security guards where I live. They stop people from getting robbed, mugged, and raped. Before they put the guards in the projects, people were getting flattened before you could wink an eye.

But then really, those guards aren't worth a penny and a half. Too many people still get killed and sometimes raped. Also we have filthy halls because people are too lazy to use the incinorator, so my father has to do it because that is his job.

Then we just had three car wrecks around our way this week, and much blood was everdent. And so there's not that much to like, but the good things, I like anyway.

THEY SAY

Running around!
Feel like moving!
Making noise gets you grooving!

Makes teachers say,
He's hyperactive.

WINOS AND JUNKIES

Winos and junkies
Laying in the street,
Can't move a muscle
Or stand on their feet.
So the winos and junkies
Get home to the bed,
And drink some wine, or take some pills,
Just to jingle up their head.

HOW THE POOR GOT POOR

Once ther was this beautiful girl who lived in and old cabin. She had old clothes and shoes. Every time that she would come out to water this one flower that she had, the rich people would say, what's a nice girl like you doing in clothes like that?

So one day, all the rich people gave her things and more things, and just kept giving her more and more. A few weeks later, the beautiful girl became very rich from all this, and the people who were rich became very poor.

Then all the people who had been so nice to her began begging for some of their things back, just so they could live again. But the girl said no, moved away, and stayed rich. And the people who were once rich stayed poor, and stayed living in Jersey City for the rest of their life.

THE EARTH

The earth is big,
and round.
Some places are dirty,
some are clean.
More places are dirty,
less are clean.
My place is dirty, in case you're asking.

THE EARTH II

The earth is a disaster,
full of sights of murder
and sounds of crying, and hurting.
I know.
I see them. I hear them.

TOMORROW

What is in the future?
Where am I going?
My mind is in darkness,
My blood stops flowing,
Just thinking about tomorrow.

Stay, today.
Stay.

THE TRIAL

The trial was held on a very hot day,
the judge was sweating like mad.
He didn't know if guilty or not,
he just put any man away.
The man was locked up for a year and a half,
he thought the judge was crazy.
The drunk that he was locked in with
said, no, he's just too lazy.

HOPELESS

Good God! THE DEATH
Good God! THE DOPE
Good God! THE WAR
Good God! NO HOPE

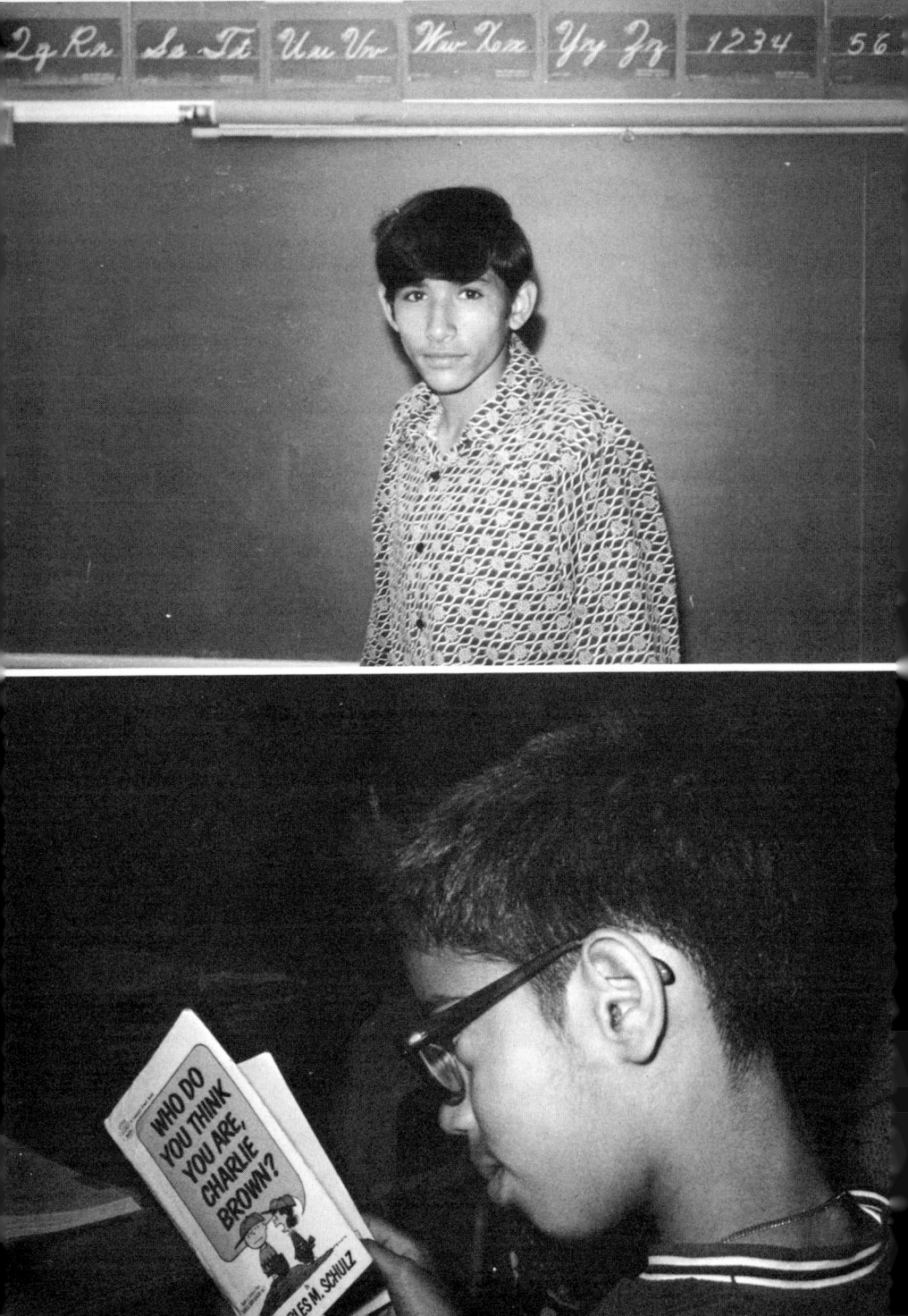

V. Jesus, 13; Debra, 11; Eusebio, 11

*". . . and I just don't think all this.
I see it, so I know it."*

THE SCHOOL GAME

The school game is fun
You may run
Very fast, but not very far.
And if you don't let things bother you,
You can almost have fun
Without winning
The school game.

LIVING

I live in Montgomery Gardens in building 4 on the 6 floor. Montgomery Gardens is not a bad place to live. You can take your turn to clear the garbage out of the hallway, and you may hear loud noises, but they go away after a while. And if you really care about your house, you can wash by your door in the hall. We do.

I WAS OLDER

I wish I was growing 4 or 3 inches a day and would hurry to be older. And there's one thing I know, and that's you have to take a lot of responsibility then. Like raising your children. And school, work, buying food, clothes, houses, cars too. And hospital care for your family.

If I was older, I would have all this responsibility. And I would be good to it.

—Debra

RIOT

It started on a Sunday
morning. There was a lot of people
starting a fight with other people
in the bar.
People were killed, and
blood was all over the street.
Houses were burned,
Cars were stolen.
I was feeling bad for the babys.

GOD

God was young for a day. He wanted to die so we could rest easy about dieing. He wanted to die so we could learn how to die. He knew that we was no good, but he died for us anyway.

They say that he was a fool. I hope not, because I been talking to him for a long time.

—Eusebio

VERY CRAZY PEOPLE

There are very crazy people in school that if they stay in class anymore, they'll get everybody crazy too. I don't like them and it's awful. I am almost going crazy too.

THE HOOK

I am a kid and I like to play the hook a lot. I don't know why I like to play the hook, unless that I think that I am getting left back and that it doesn't do no good to come to school. But if I knew what was going on in school I wouldn't play the hook no more. There is nothing to do on the hook anyway.

—Jesus

JUST NEXT DOOR

This lady, she lived just next door to me. She was asleep in the dark. At night, someone came to her house to rape and kill her. This happened to her once before. She be so scared, she went crazy. And so the lady jumped from the 3 floor window and died.

That is why you sure better keep your lights on.

When people push you around, you feel bad. When you get scolded by them, you want to yell back, and inside you want to kill them. But yelling will get you nothing, and killing will get you in trouble. So if you can, you should just shut your mouth and go away. Because some people don't care. They will stab you and walk away happy.

—*Eusebio*

A GOOD SCHOOL

A good school should help us learn about the other world.

MY DREAMS

One day I dreamed that this man he came into our house with a knife and he took my sister and shook and stabbed her to death. And then he cut her into pieces. I would throw these dreams out of my head, but I can't.

—*Eusebio*

GIRLS

When I go out with a girl, I like to do a lot of things. I show off. I like it. It give me a chance to talk, and to be big.

LIVING HERE

I don't like living here because I think that there are a lot of man who take dope. And also kid that take dope and all those things.

And I don't think it. I see it so I know it.

—Jesus

MAD

When I'm mad, I feel like kicking someone or something. I be thinking of what bad things I could do. I think of fighting people, of never going home, of hitting my sister.

THE WONDER

As I softly sleep in my bed,
A wonder comes to me.
It refuses to tell me what it wants.
Many wonders come to me,
But this one is unusual.
It is about freedom.

But as I begin to follow it,
It runs from me, from my grasp,
And from my mind.

—Debra

WITHOUT FRIENDS

I like to stay with friends, and when they move I feel bad because then I am alone outside. It is no fun. Just hanging around the house is bad because there is nothing to do. All you can do is stay inside. And I got just a little room.

I like my building because people there are free, nice, and happy sometimes. They are not like others around who take dope. Those people are really stupid. But it is not really their fault. I wish that they would never say dope through the TV, because now people know all about it.

—*Eusebio*

RAIN

All the time when I go out and it be raining my friends will always ask why does it rain. And some will say that Mary god's wife is ringing the water out of her wash, or that the river up there ran over, or that the angels be crying. But I know that this is not true. I know that there is something more to it. I would really like to know who rain is, and why he does that thing he does.

MONEY

If I had money, I would buy me a house, and cars, clothes, food, coats, boats, shoes, and everything else I need. I would buy 100 maids, 100 cooks, and 100 servants. Then I would buy myself a big piece of ham.

—Debra

MY BROTHER

My brother was very sick. He looked bad and got very bony. He stunk in bed, and his tongue was colored. And when he fell asleep, he was calling for me.

GROWING UP

Some kids grow up good,
But some
Just like to be
Old, and broke, and dirty
Just like everyone else.
I see it all,
But it's not me.
Not me.

—Eusebio

GOING

No matter where I go, I always feel like I am still home. But then whenever I go somewhere, I make like that I am going to P.R. I tell my mother and she say that I am going nowhere. And to stop my stupid ideas.

FREE

Free free
I am free
The world is big and I am small
But I am
Still free

—Jesus

SAD, WITH NOTHING

I wish that all people were happy. But some people are sad with nothing their own. They old raggerty things, they just live in an old house with no food. They live with no family and no neighborhood. Just their own sad self.

WAR

I think that there is war because other people are in danger somewhere. We don't know about it here, because in the U.S. we are almost free and not that much in danger. It is good here. Other places are dying.

—Eusebio

MY PERSON

I'm an unusual person. I don't know what kind of a person, but I do strange things. Like dreaming things, and when I wake up I still be in the dream. And other things too. Every day in school I do strange things, like daydreaming horrible things about myself and believing it.

UNLOVED

To feel unloved is like to be alone in the dark. No talking, no noise, no laughing. No one there, everyone out. In the house alone. Nothing to do or even to think about. Unloved.

—Debra

THE NIGHT

The night is very scary when you are alone in the house. It becomes dark, and brown. And your eyes rush around looking for nothing, and your mind wants a crowd.

DEATH

When someone dies in a family,
we call it death.
And then we say that his death
occured on April 10, 1971 or something,
and he goes into a hole.
And that is what death is all about.

—*Eusebio*

THE CITY

The city is a nice place to live. I live in Jersey City and I like it. I think that you would like living here too. Because I feel that soon we are going to stop messing the place up, and bring ourselves together. Then I will love the city even more.

Dear Mr. Duva,
This may not be a poem, but it show how
I care about the city. Thank you.
—Debra

WAKING UP

I was home.
I went to sleep.
I woke up.
And I went outside.

Sleep was better.

—Jesus

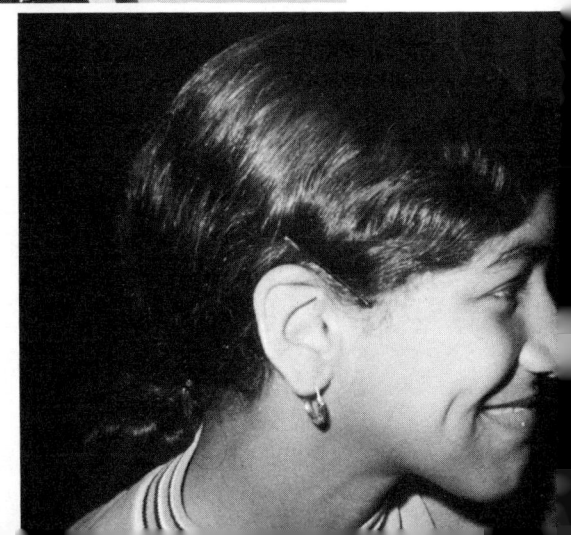

VI. Ramon, 12; Eida, 11; Michele, 13; Gil 13

*". . . It's all too loud.
There's no quietness for your ear anytime."*

MY HOUSE

Well I live in a house that is almost falling down. It is right here on the corner by the school. My room is sorry too. You can tell where my room is at night because my light is right by the window. If you want to look.

—Ramon

NOISE

Sometimes my friend's mother and father be outside fighting. They be so loud you can hear them way down the street. And when they be finished, everybody talks about them.

But my aunt has the biggest mouth in the building. She calls me so loud I feel like running away. My sister's baby cries so loud you can't hear yourself talk.

It's all loud, too loud. There's no quietness for your ear anytime.

GOING OUT

I feel like a fool when me and my friends go out. They go to a store and steal everything they can and I feel very bad, because it feels like I did it. I feel like a dog that's been sick as a dog for years.

—Michele

LOVE

My mother bought me
A gold ring,
A ring that says LOVE on it.
But everybody thinks
It's not real.

GOING

    When I am with my friends, I feel alright. But I got to move to P.R. That is too bad. I have to leave you, all my friends where I live at. I told Olga to give me one of her picture because I'm not going to see her anymore. But I will write to her. I am sorry I won't see you anymore my friends. I am right now trying very hard not to cry.

—Eida

MY FRIENDS

They like to get you in trouble. They stick with you until trouble comes. They pull fire alarms, and I get blamed for it. They rob and steal stuff, so I also have friends in jail. Like Shorty for kicking a cop.

Pete, Porgy, Anton, Jaimie, Jesus. These are my friends. I got all kinds. Fat, skinny, and crazy friends, like Gilbert. I go with them because they know what to look for. They know if there's anything to do.

WHAT WILL HAPPEN TO ME

Jail will happen to me. I might be in jail with Jose. I might get married, MIGHT. I might get a job, MIGHT. I always wanted to drive a helicopter. Or maybe be one of those men who drive the suitcases to the plane. It must be nice being up in the air and far. I always wanted to be far.

—*Gil*

WHY I PRAY

I pray because I like god. That is why I pray. God's mind helps you when you get in trouble. God's mind helps you on the street and you don't know it. He always thinks about the streets.

SLEEP

I like to sleep because your body needs to rest. All day long you scream about your father or your girlfriend or your mother. But to sleep and rest from everything this is good for you.

—Ramon

NEIGHBORHOOD SOUNDS

My neighborhood sounds are sad:
The sound of the wind pushing junk around,
The scream of a kid getting jumped on the street,
Or the cry of a baby on a bus.

CAROL

    Carol is my girl friend. She is a very nice girl. But she gets on my back sometimes. And I don't like her when she drinks.

—Michele

FAKE LOVE

I think to really love is good for you. But some love is not real. People live with a girl without love and I know it. I know girls that live with a boy even though they saying to everybody that they don't like him.

Around my way they have a lot of fights. They like to take people money. They like to break in people houses to get their furniture. They won't let you live quiet.

—*Eida*

FAITH

I don't have much faith in anything. I don't know a thing about god, I never went to church. If you live around my way, you are in hell already anyway. So I never think to go to church. But I guess what god is is someone to bless you or if you wish or something, to make it come true. Then when you die you can be up there with the angels and all those little babies around.

MY OWN SCHOOL

If a school was mine it would be an old school with psychedelic windows. Green and red lights on. You would do whatever you want there like smoke in the bathroom and drink beer in the back of the class. And you would go home anytime you want. There would be no more books, and you would do all your work in school, not home. And mostly you would be allowed to play in the closet.

—Gil

GOD

Well I think that god, this is a good person. He is a person that thinks about the world. And he cares for the world more than the world cares for him.

HELP

Well this is serious. One day I was walking around when I heard somebody say HELP, she just said HELP. I ran because it was so scary the way she said it. So I ran home. The next day the news said that some girl got in trouble and died there.

—Ramon

IF I WERE RICH

If I were rich, this would be a very short story. Because I am no good with money.

MYSELF

I am a girl. I don't do no hard dope and no pot. And I'm thin and very tall for my age. I never brag about myself, like to say I have creamy skin. My brother always calls me skinny and makes me mad. My mother told me to stop growing, but what could I do?

—*Michele*

THE END

This boy was tease this girl,
And the girl said you better
Stop it before you get slap down.
And then he didn't tease the girl no more,
He just loved her, and held it all inside.

The rocket went up
In the sky today.

SLEEP

I sleep all night in bed,
And I wake up in the morning.
I'm growing everyday,
And wakink in the morning.
And nothing changes.

—Eida

MY BUILDING

In my building there are people I know very good. They're friendly and nice, but sometimes they're something else. They be in the hall calling names at each other, being very fresh. They break people windows, and put fires in the halls.

And that lady Mrs. Johnson, she is bad and noisy and nosey. She come in the hall and be throwing water on the boys sitting there. Mrs. Johnson is the next door neighbor to me. She comes to my house and says I opened your mail, Michele. I thought it was mine because you and me have the same last name.

—Michele

LOVE

Love is like you want somebody real good. Somebody to do anything for. And no more fighting, shooting, stabbing. There would be peace in the world. Peace and love and safety in the world.

DARKNESS

At night when it gets darker and darker, it gets worse and worse. And the blacker that you are, the worse it gets. Because sometimes they can't find you in the night.

—*Gil*

ALONE

When you're alone, you usually get afraid of something. Nobody to talk to. Feeling bad and worried. Well I feel that way.

When I'm lonely, I might go to the river by myself and watch the water and the boats. Or I might go home and just sit there. And every little noise, I jump. And I think about things that are easy to forget.

—Gil

VII. Jose L., 11; Cheryl, 12; Jose R., 12; Della, 11

" . . . *I do all that I can,*
but mostly I make mistakes in my life."

THE DREAM

I was dreaming
in my mother's stomach
that on June 5 or 6,
I would be born.
June 2 went by,
and 4 and 5.
Then on June 6, I got out of there;
Into life,
and another dream.

—Cheryl

MORE THAN NOTHING

You think that dope is nothing? Dope is more than nothing. Dope is cool, yes I know, but don't you see that it can curse your life. Dope is bad, very bad. Some have died. Some will die.

AROUND

People taking dope, not knowing what to do. Not knowing who to trust or turn to with troubles. Always stealing, then running away, and stealing again. Then crying for no reason at all.

Around here is mad. There are schools, buses, cars, and sadness. There are parks, jails, bums, stoops, alleys. The city has dope, but no hope

—Jose R.

MONEY

They say that money is clean,
but to me it's unfriendly.

PEOPLE

People is what the world is made of.
Not just people,
But others.

—Della

DEATH BY LOVE

When your heart
Dies of love,
It doesn't die of the pain,
Or the hurt.
It dies of the calm.

IN THE RIVER

My friend was jumping
in the river.
The sun was shining,
the birds
were singing.
But the rats were waiting
because he was drowning,
and screaming a prayer.

—Jose L.

THAT BELL

That bell!
A good one at 3:15,
a bad one at 8:30,
when our oldest and most respected teachers
stand and yell in the hallways:
come on, people, you late!
As if we didn't know.
That bell! That horrible bell!
That bell,
and that YELL!

I live in the funky, crowded, stinken city. And my mother says when a whole lot of people get together it ain't going to be nothing but a lot of fighting, killing, and commotion. That's why we are going down south for the summer, and when we come back, we will move to Dayton, Ohio. And if that is no better, I don't know what I'll do.

—*Cheryl*

TENEMENT HOUSE

I wish that I knew more about being a tenement house. Who knows what they are doing or thinking. For all we know they could be planning to take over the world. But that's crazy.

THINKING

I think that I think
when I think, "do I think?",
yes I think!
That's what I think.
I think.

—Jose R.

GRIEF

Grief means death.
It means sorrow,
And sadness.
Darkness and loneliness
And empty streets,
That's grief.

LUNCH

Bar-B-Que potato chips,
Candy hats, licorice sticks,
Salty pretzels, can of coke,
Sour balls, and cigarette smoke.

Slurp, puff, crunch—
That's lunch.

—Della

BEST FRIENDS

Some of my best friends are really good with me. Some of them even let me use money when I need money to use. Some of my friends are junkies, but if somebody be hitting me, they help me hit them back. And they like to steal things.

But when we are in the river, we promise each other that we won't steal our stuff while we are swimming. And most of the time we don't. And that is why it is good sometimes to have best friends.

STEAL

People go uptown to steal mostly. They jump whites and their friends and take their bikes and money. And they go crying to their house. I feel sorry for them, but you know whites sometimes are bad people. The police like to lock up the black people and the spanish people when they steal, but not the white people. But the black and spanish people are still strong. They steal like Robin Hood steal.

—*Jose L.*

RABBIT

This was my friend. His name was Rabbit. That was his name because of something he did a long time ago, I don't know what. Rabbit would go into the world every day of his life, even though he was very sick. He was a junkie, and he knew that he was sick. But he did not tell anyone because he did not want to upset them.

One day Rabbit went into the world and he felt extra sick. He fell into the street. 2 hours later, somebody picked him up, then put him back down. He was dead.

—Jose R.

NIGHT

The day turns into night,
The darkness swallows the light,
The stars no longer shining bright,
The moon no longer burning white,
Total darkness when
The black man meets the night.

NATURE

Nature is warm,
Nature is beautiful—
I love nature's taste.

—Della

ME

I am a boy that makes mistakes,
a boy who wears glasses.
I am a medium boy
in a medium city.
I do all that I can,
but mostly I make mistakes
In my life.

ABOUT DRUGS

   I see some of my friends taking drugs. I hear them talking about it. I think that drugs are no good for people. They asked me if I wanted to taste, but I said no thanks I am not going to be a junkie in my life. I want to go to work and not be caught by the police for doing this or that.
   I want to have peace. I want to live in my life.

—*Jose L.*

WHERE I LIVE

Now the incinerator is broken, and everynight I have to take garbage downstairs to where they burn it. There are people down there who steal and try to sell it to other people. And if you don't buy, they break into your house when you're out and steal and wreck your whole house. They even take what's in your refrigerator. Mostly only drug addicts do it. I hate to bring the garbage downstairs.

I live in the Montgomery Projects. One good thing about it is that nobody and I mean nobody in the projects is conceited. If they try acting like it, everybody knows that they're crazy if they think they're better. Because if they were better, they wouldn't be living in the dumpy projects. Everybody there knows what spot they're in. You can see it by the expressions on their faces.

—Cheryl

FRIENDS

My friends are nice. They don't really look for trouble. They mind their own business, and they do what they want to do. They smoke pot and leave home mostly. They say for me to try it, but I say nothing doing. I say nothing can beat my girl, and she's clean with not even sniffing glue.

I know that they don't really want to take that stuff, and I know they try to stop, but they hook on it. So I just say to them you can smoke your pot and pop your pills and sniff your glue, but nothing can beat my girl.

—Jose R.

THE VILLAIN

I saw a villain man,
He was beating on a lady down the street.
And when he finished, he ran away.
A policeman ran after him,
Caught him at the corner, and shot him.
Down at the corner, between York and Montgomery Street,
The villain died.

SOME LIKE YOU AND SOME DON'T

    Some people like me because sometimes I am nice. Some people hate me because sometimes I am nasty. That's why sometimes life is good, and sometimes life is bad. Some people say that life is good or bad by where you are or how rich you are. But I know it's by if you be nasty or nice.

—Jose L.

SCHOOL IN THE RAIN

As I walked to school today in the rain, I knew it was not going to be a very good day. Walking up the school steps, I just knew it would be bad. A dreary day. A dark, dark day. And I wondered if there was some way I could help it end. I have no use for dark days.

IN THE CITY

In the city are people who fight against pollution, and people who make pollution. There are people who work, and people who don't work. There are too many babies born, and too many who die.

In the city are people who push dope, and people who prevent it. In the city are many things. All of them fighting each other.

—Cheryl

WHEN I DIE

I'd like flowers,
and sunshine.
Grass growing,
leaves blowing,
dogs barking.
Nothing stopping, everything the same,
when I die.

—Jose L.

VIII. Rosemary, 11

". . . Even when I am in bed at night I think of all this."

It would be very funny
to find that I am not really me.

CLOUDS

Clouds are like people
Who move mysteriously about;
They are different from each other,
But as stubborn as the next.
Turning dark, they cry,
Getting clear again, they fill with sun,
And gain simplicity.

WRONG

I knew a black bear
That went to war,
Because a white judge
Told him to.
That same bear's white friend
Didn't go,
Because the white judge
Didn't tell him so.
And that black bear was my brother.

MY BUILDING

My building is really crazy. People party all night when other people have to go to work in the morning. Nobody gets what sleep they should anyway. Sometimes the hall smells shitty and damp. When the light on the 3 floor is out, you are afraid to go upstairs because sometimes men be hiding back there, ready to jump out.

DEATH

As the stars were glistening,
I got shot.
Now I am on a beach,
with no one here to rescue me.
The wind slowly comes,
and the water tries to wash my wounds.
The sand is like a blanket,
trying to warm me.
Slowly the sky turns from mid to morn—
the sun comes out!
I'm dead.

1:36 PM 6/23/71
HOW I FEEL RIGHT NOW

I feel as if something new is about to occur. As if I have been locked up in a chain of lies, and am about to escape. I feel like writing all the time right now, telling you about it. I feel the blood rushing up to my head. I feel tired. Not tired, exhausted and heavy.

I feel a little dizzy, as if I have had a good time all these years. I feel that I should do something terrible, like commit a murder to myself and write a mysterious letter to back it up. I feel the rushing of water, and the wind behind my back. That tired feeling is back again, as if I have been writing my whole 11 years without stopping. Also, I feel the urge to kill.

Now, all of a sudden, I fell lonely.

TIRED

When I'm tired I feel so weary as if I have been working all day and night. My arms feel as if I have been holding up the sky for 210 years. My legs feel as if I have been running from jail for murder. My head feels like it has been dropped107timees.

My body feels the pain and exhaustion of tireness. My eyes feel as if they have been jumping rope all day without stopping. My heart feels sick of pumping, it feels so weak. My whole self feels as if it is ready to collapse with nobody awake enough to help it up. I told my mother how I felt and she said that's nothing because her and my father feel like that most all the time.

TONGUE

    What is red as red could be
is it inside of me?
Can I see it,
can it see me?
Do I have three?
    What is red as red could be
that talks the hell out of me?
Can it be seen,
is it clean?
Can it be very, very mean?
    What is red with pimples on it
that talks the hell out of me?

BLACKPIE

I am a pie
that bakes all day.
They leave me in the oven
to turn black all day.
The white man, before he bakes me,
beats me, and rolls me till I'm flat—
then he pops me in an oven
to turn blacker and blacker all day.

FRIENDS

Sometimes I feel that I don't have a friend in the world. At other times, I feel that I have too many. Sometimes they don't want to be bothered with me, and I feel all bad and mistreated. I feel that I would like certain people to be dead, then at other times I don't.

Often my friends tease me. Like when they say that I always have to wear braids. Also, some of my friends pick on younger kids just because they have older brothers and sisters to back them up. In this way, my feelings about my friends are "negative". But sometimes my friends are good to have. They bother you, but they don't mean it. Like when you get something new, they say your mother just found her welfare check, or your father hit the number. But if you get hurt, they will stay with you until you stop bleeding.

My mother says pick your friends out carefully. She says they can do you awful bad sometimes. Even when I am in bed at night I think of all this.

GOD

God I have never seen, but have heard of. They say he does a lot of wonderful things, and I believe it too. Sometimes when I see something horrible, I always pray to keep it away from my mother, and usually it does.

But when I ask for something and it doesn't happen, I always scream there is no god. But then I think for a minute, and I say I'm sorry to the air. And I know that he hears me.

My mother wakes me up early every Sunday, and I go to church. And when I sit there, I feel that god doesn't want anything to do with me. But then at times I feel like I am up there with him.

MERRY-GO-ROUND

When children are on the merry-go-round,
the ponies get fast, and strong.
As the children laugh and shout about,
the ponies go round and round.
But as they get off,
the ponies get soft,
and the little children cry.

FEELING

I feel wrong about things sometimes. I feel depressed about certain things, things that people do. And about myself, I sometimes feel unwanted. I wonder why bad things always happen to me. I feel that magic or good luck is a phoney because it never happens to me.

I sometimes wish that I would never have to grow up. At night I cry because my conscience tells me a lot of wierd things. When 12:00 comes and I go to the lunchroom, I always feel kind of lonely. Sometimes when I cut my hand, I feel as if I did it on purpose. Inside me is emptiness.

WHO I AM

I am a black man,
stiff and cold.
My friends, they're so bold,
they left me to die,
die in the war, so cruel and cold.
Left me to die,
with no shoes on my feet.
But the white man, they helped him,
they fear him,
they're sweet.

MY PEOPLE

My people always rush about
and get in trouble, through the night
and die, before their time.
They always shout, and scream, and
you can't stop them—
because it's their day,
and they go out to die.

IX. Randy, 12; Priscilla, 11; Darlene, 12; Jackie, 11

"The people around do so many things . . . I don't even bother to look no more."

WHERE AM I GOING

Where am I going?
I'm going to work,
have a job,
be a wife.
Where am I going?
I'm going somewhere
where I can bring up my children
where there's no dirt,
where there's no dirt at all.
I am going away,
somewhere else,
and grow up again.

—Darlene

SUMMER

In the summer, I feel awful, terrible, rediculous, sticky, hot, exhausted, can't get around, not able to talk, can't hardly breathe, stuffy nose, watery eyes. What a terrible feeling. Like a dirty pillow over your face.

CARING

What's the matter with this world?
Doesn't anyone care anymore?
But what's the sense of trying to help
When no one wants it?

Somewhere in this world, at least some people
must be trying to care.
Trying and crying their hearts away.

—Darlene

NOT SO BAD

It's not so bad where I live. When you need help with something, the people I know will help you. And if you have a problem, they try to figure it out with you.

Every Wednesday, the street cleaners come and they clean all the dirt up and they wash the ground. My people walk down the street with really colorful clothes on.

NOT SO GOOD

It's not so good where I live. One day when I was coming in the house, five boys were in the hall. I heard them talking, but didn't know what about. Then I saw them shooting into one boy's arm. That boy fell to the floor. I ran and told someone, but I forget who.

Then the police and the hospital cane, and they said the boy was dead. The other boys were arrested I guess. So it's not so good around my house.

—*Priscilla*

BORED

Looking for a job,
Can't find one.
And when you do, it's a joke;
You don't want it.

GROW UP

In the chair with diapers. Can't do nothing but eat. Your mother comes and takes care of you. You is crying and crying for everything you want. Nothing seems to please you. All the days through, winter passes, and summer. You wait. You want to grow up to a man and do for yourself.

—Randy

WHO AM I

Am I the bird that sits in the tree,
Or the ant that crawls all day?

No, I am just the girl who
Goes to school every day,
But nobody knows.
Nobody knows,
And nobody cares.

OUR FLAT IS HOT

Our flat is hot
On a summer day—
To the park so cool,
We run away.

But Fall is coming,
I can smell it—
All the grass is dusty.

—Jackie

THE HALL

When I was small,
I'd play in the hall.
Now I've grown tall,
And just walk through the hall,
Carefully.

THE HALL II

There are dark hallways where I live. When you go in, you get scared. Voices scream stop stop. Then it's quiet again. You don't wonder what happened. You just know that you might be next, so you hurry upstairs.

—*Darlene*

WHY I'M AFRAID

One night when I was going on an errand to get chinese food I went down this dark street. There I saw rats, cats, dogs, and lots of crazy people around. This one man he came to me and he said are you going somewhere down the street. I said yes. He said that I wouldn't if I were you. I said why, but he didn't say anything, he just walked away.

So I stood there saying should I or shouldn't I. I went down the street, and I saw a dead man laying in the street, and another man was coming at me with blood on his hands and his face. I ran and I ran and I ran until I got home and at my house they said where's the chinese food.

—Priscilla

PUNISH ME

Once they made me salute the flag in school 20 times because I did something.

THE JOKE

I went to the store and saw some boys jump an old man and take his money. And beat him. They took a bottle and hit him upside his head. He was calling for help, but nobody helped him. He got up off the ground and was crying that nobody wanted to help him. He went to the river and he was keeping his eye on the river and he jumped into the river and killed his selve. It was terrible, but people be telling the story like it was a big joke.

—Randy

MOST EVERYTHING

Around here, there are all sorts of houses. Tall, short, dirty, clean, junky, all in place. There are all sorts of kids. Bad, good, selfish, proud. And there are all sorts of germs too. Lockjaw, mouth germ, and many more germs and diseases. Around here is most everything.

THE LITTLE BOY AND THE RAT

I knew this little boy who always played with rats. One day he saw a big rat and he slammed it with a stick. The rat squealed and bled, and limped away.

—Darlene

WHO AM I?

I am a person who is very soft-hearted and happy. As a matter of fact, there are only three things that upset me: air pollution, dope, and war. These I hate.

I am a person who believes in love. I believe that love can give you the mind to think beautiful thoughts even though your eyes see horrible things around you.

I am also sometimes very touchy. Like when I am trying to do something, and someone is making noise. Then I can get really mad. Like now, I wish that Rose would stop talking.

—*Priscilla*

JERSEY CITY

Jersey City is a sorry place.
I don't like the way it talks to me.
I don't like the way it looks at me.
I don't like the way it lives.

PRIVATE

I like to be alone, in private, to think about things and myself. I wish that I was in a place that was quiet. Quiet and private, and alone.

—*Jackie*

THINGS

Many things happen around my way where I live. The people do so many things. They be in the hallway taking dope. And sometimes they die from dope. They go around and steal cars and sell them. And they beat on you if you talk about it. All this is done quick and a lot. I don't even bother to look no more.

INSIDE ME

I don't know what is inside my body and what makes me do the things I do. I don't know why I wake up in the morning, and why I feel good or bad. Sometimes I talk to my selve. I don't know how come I do that. But it is nothing. Everybody do it when they alone.

—Randy

THE CITY

The city is a place where you can get things done faster. If you lived in the country, you would probably have to walk 5 miles just to go shopping or anything else.

But one thing more. In the country, chances are the store would be there when you got there. Here in the city, you never know.

THIS MAN

This man was kind of crazy,
He always acted lazy;
His wife and kids just cried and cried,
So he drank
Until he died.

—Priscilla

PLAYING BALL

Sometime everyday I go outside and I have my basketball with me. Me and my friends be playing basketball. And I be hot on the court. I be popping from right to left. And when I have the lead right in the middle of the game some boys come. And they say can I have a shot brother. Come on can I dig, only one shot. I thought we was pals, man. I be saying in my mind a shot or I get my butt kicked, that's what you mean. Pals. I don't even Know them. Some pals.

WILSON

Wilson aways wants people to steal out of the stores for him. He even steals money out of his mothers pocket just to get some dope. He tells his mother that he got to have money for lunch. She finally give it to him and he say he be right back. He takes the money and go get some dope. He always sick a little later. His mother says she can't take it no more.

—Randy

ME

I am a person,
and I must be special.
My friends want me around,
and my boyfriend says I'm a real good thing.

THE EDGE

The edge is almost like the end,
and you can't tell when that edge,
when that end,
will come;
when
your world will end.

—*Priscilla*

HELPLESS

Unable to do anything about pollution,
can't stop a murder.
Can't save an empty lot from garbage,
or a tree from rotting away.
Can't do a thing about it by myself,
and there's almost nothing green anymore.
Nothing white, or black.
Everything gray.

UNDERSTAND

Do you understand why we have wars? Do you understand why people are dying? Do you understand the hating and hitting and hurting in the street? I'm tired of seeing people dying I'm tired of seeing people sick. I'm tired of killing. Can you explain it to me? I want to understand.

—Darlene

MY WORK

My work is based on things that have happened to me in the past. Now days people are talking about how they want to be poets. They know that when you resight a poem, you become filled with love. And everyone wants that. When I write, I want that love too.

POLLUTION

How do I feel about pollution? Well I'll tell you one thing, I'd rather die a natural death than die of pollution. And we got to fight pollution with our minds. We can't use the guns, sticks, and knives that we usually do our fighting with.

—*Priscilla*

THE THINGS THAT I SAY

I say some things that I mean, and some that I don't mean. And they can tell you all about me. But if you don't be around me enough, you will not hear the things that I say. And you will not know me at all.

—*Randy*

Afterword

The entries in this book appear exactly as written. Minor grammatical corrections have been made only where they would not interfere with the characteristic music of the children's voices. They have been grouped for presentation according to author.

By way of introduction, only the age of the writer is offered. Photographs of the children are placed at random throughout the book. All family names, where mentioned, have been changed.

Nothing is mentioned of any personal problems, family difficulties, or other specific situations that may exist for the children in their daily lives. I truly believe that their work speaks, shouts, for and about them loudly enough.

There are many friends without whose help these writings would still be forgotten pieces of sixth-grade classwork. Acknowledgment and thanks should go to several of the more special ones.

To Janet Piechocki, for her sensitivity; to Richard

Savulich, for his editorial skills; to Daniel Sohmer, for his advice; to Robert Dziekonski, for his power with line and design. To the parents of the children, for their cooperation; to the faculty of the Kennedy School, for their emotion.

And I thank, most of all, Sarah S. Hallahan and Dr. Francis J. McCarthy who, knowing how I felt about the children of the city, let me teach.